Kemet

Awakening

Kemet

Awakening

A Resurgence of African Thought

RUNESU CHAZVEMBA

Copyright © 2021 Runesu Chazvemba
All rights reserved

ISBN 13: 978-0-620-98438-6 (Softcover)

The characters and events portrayed in this book are fictitious. Any similarity to real persons, living or dead, is coincidental and not intended by the author.

No part of this book may be reproduced, stored in a retrieval system, or transmitted in any form or by any means, electronic, mechanical, photocopying, recording, or otherwise, without the express written permission of the publisher.

To order additional copies of this book, contact

Aqua Quill Publishing
A division of Blue Flame Lily (Pty) Ltd
+27 722329269

aquaquillpublishing@gmail.com

To my poetry fans, friends, and family around the world.

I am in debt to my family for their unwavering support along the way, my wife Natalie and daughters, Xenia and Nyasha, for their contributions to this writing; their beauty and spontaneity were just a help in inspiring my creative side to blossom and flourish.

This writing would not have been possible without their constant urging on and a helping hand when the muses faltered, they stoked the flames of imagination to no end.

When Africa in sleep rose in the night of Beulah, and bound down the Sun & Moon. His friends cut his strong chains, & overwhelmed his dark Machines in fury & destruction, and the Man reviving repented, he wept before his wrathful brethren, thankful & considerate for their well-timed wrath. But Albion's sleep is not like Africa's, and his machines are woven with his life; nothing but mercy can save him! Nothing but mercy interposing. Lest he should slay Jerusalem in his fearful jealousy.

William Blake, Jerusalem

Contents

Contents 8
Foreword 14
Preface 15
Introduction 17
Chapter One 20
    Poems of Hope 20
Kemet Awakening 2
    A Time of Glory 3
    A Glorious World 5
The Eternal Land 9
The death of intellect 13
Enraptured Dreams 8
    Unfurling Wings 21
    The Impeccable Quarry 23
    The Immortal Wanderers 27
In Art Immortalised 30
Ignorance Unveiled 34
    In Kemet 38
Chapter Two 40

Poems of Resolve	40
The Sentry	41
Solitude	48
Indigence of the Soul	50
Emptiness	52
A Metamorphosis	58
The Black Prometheus	62
Ruins	64
In Search of Glory	68
Renewal	71
Chapter Three	74
Universe of the Mind	74
All a Dream	75
A Mirror Reflection	77
Upon the Crucifix	78
Upon a Pawn	79
Crude Sculpture	80
Superstitious Murmurs	82
Receding Glory	83
The Dark Rider	84
The Profligates	85
Thought Pollution	86
Dirge of the Ancients	87
The Gift of Sight	88

- Tortured Pain ... 90
  - The Red World ... 91
  - The Brightest Star ... 93
- Draw the Curtains ... 95
  - Writers Block ... 96
  - Conversations with Judas ... 97
  - The Modern Cave ... 99
  - Nostalgia ... 100
  - The Unravelling Searing Dream ... 101
  - Time Receding ... 102
  - Befuddled Senses ... 103
  - Grandeur ... 104
  - Fading Flame ... 106
  - The Mind Dancing ... 107
  - Raging Emotions ... 109
  - The Mind Awakening ... 110
  - The Man of Ideas ... 111
  - Integrated Man ... 112
  - Within the Cranium ... 114
  - Wisdom of the Ancients ... 115
  - A Symbol ... 116
  - The Storming of Heaven ... 118
- The Ascendance ... 119
  - The Mirror Within ... 121

A Hand	123
Kemet Awakening	125
About the Author	126
Glossary	127
Books by This Author	129
Index	136
Image Credits	139

"We, in our sighs and murmurs in the wind, carved,
The world in valleys and mountains as we willed
We are builders of vast universes,
The artists for each aesthetic expression in nature.
And in the world exhibited in flagrant abandon,
Of a texture and structure overflowing with beauty,
When doubt assails cock your head back,
And into the infinite cosmos unflinchingly stare,
For the grandeur above in all its astonishing beauty,
Is yours made with an unbridled flare of the ineffable,
That yet weaves a tapestry of magnificence,
In the fabric of the cosmos, an eternal jewel.
To bedazzle all generations to come with beauty,
Unequalled by anything ever in man's dreams imagined,"

A Glorious World

R Chazvemba

Foreword

Echoes of Kemet has been penned with raw emotion. Be prepared to *feel* your way through each poem in each categorised chapter. These are "Poems of Hope", "Poems of Resolve" and "Universe of the Mind". This sure does pique your interest.

Runesu Chazvemba explores the abovementioned subjects through poetry from a distinctly Grand African (Pre-European) perspective, that is, from the time when Africa housed great civilisations centuries ago.

The author espouses the belief in Africa's potential for greatness if it can overcome its challenges and gives voice to how Africa can rise.

Besides emotive streams of insight and entertainment, you will be introduced to a colourful, intellectual vocabulary.

- Natalie Ann Fajer-Chazvemba, Published Author
- 29 November 2021

Preface

I stumbled upon a dewdrop on a chrysanthemum leaf once, it was early in the morning on my way to a lecture. The sun hung low in the eastern skies. A beam of light had caught the dewdrop, and there where they touched, there it was a rainbow in all its majestic colourful form, albeit in a microcosm. I marvelled at the beauty and sublimity of it all. I had only a few minutes to spare before the lecture commenced, nevertheless, I could not help but kneel and imbibe in that one spectacular moment. It was a transient scene that left such a strong impression on all my faculties.

There is so much beauty in the world that goes unacknowledged. I resolved then to capture the aesthetics of the world in words. The poems in this collection and others I have written are an effort to encapsulate that sublimity in a form that posterity might appreciate. The whispers of blades of grass, the wide expanses of a verdant scene, the misty hues of craggy mountain peaks, the laughter of a toddler, the swirls of floral dresses of maidens, the pulse of human interactions and the twinkling glory in the firmaments, all and more serve as inspiration for poetic expression.

The poems in this collection are broadly categorised into three main areas: Poems of Hope, Poems of Resolve, and The Universe of the Mind. It is often thought that nature stands in mute silence, amorphous and insentient; however, in paying attention to the world around us and finding interest in a blade of grass and a glassy skyscraper towering to the heavens, it dawned upon me that we infuse the world with meaning and beauty if we so wish. This work is an invitation to partake in the creation of the world in thoughts, emotions, and words. May the enterprise be an exciting one!

R Chazvemba November 29, 2021

Introduction

Other Worlds Untold and *Whispers of the Dark Race* are the two poetry anthologies to which this current writing is a sequel. This work can veritably be considered to be the ultimate expression of feeling, thought, and consciousness. Recognising the supremacy of consciousness in the manifestation of the physical universe, the identity of this consciousness can only be shown through the abstract, the woof and warp of the creative spring. The poems in this writing are divided into three chapters: Poems of Hope, Poems of Resolve, and the Universe of the Mind. What was imagined before can be seen captured in architecture, sculptures, and other artistic expressions of the past.

Africa has been plagued by a plethora of challenges spanning half a millennium. In this book, one learns to identify some of those challenges but, as though by alchemy, transforms the sordidness of such a past into something of grandeur and beauty. In ancient Kemet, the phoenix was venerated as a symbol of regeneration, of resurrection, and transcending the strictures of the corporeal. The poems in this work, albeit vicariously, transport the audience through the primordial murky waters of creation to the ascension of the human consciousness to the infinite azure of the vast heavenly dome.

The famed philosopher of near contemporary times posited that, "Everything in thought is preceded by physical action." Therefore, Homo sapiens sapiens in his current state is a summation of a million years of contact with the physical universe from the distant and fading memories of Ardipithecus coming down the ages to Australopithecus, Homo genus and modern humans with his surfeit of intrigue, brutality and space age technology we have broadened our experiences beyond this universe.

This book brings out this concept, that even in the midst of the worst maelstrom, there resides a glimmer of light which a little fanning with the breath of our minds can be transformed into a conflagration of sublime experiences. The beauty of existence, the facility of human creativity to fashion a world full of magic and infinite possibilities.

Chapter One
Poems of Hope

Hope springs eternal in the human breast;
Man, never is, but always to be blest.

-Alexander Pope (1688-1744) *Essay on Man*

Kemet Awakening

Out of the desert that covers
The land from coast to coast
The mound that splits
The vast expanses of the ocean
A terrain long and undulating
Stretching from pole to pole
In incensed fury, the spirits of the land
Like a thousand lions roar.

Straining at the sturdy chains
That binds them to the bowels of the land
A whirlwind tempestuous spins,
Cleaving the very earth in two
Setting free the pent-up fury,
Of a million years at abeyance,
Africa, this chained and yoked giant
Unravels towering to the heavens!

Its shadow long to girdle the loins
From end to end of the earth
The time of the slumber is past
And the darkness of eons lifts,
In torment of a million years in confinement
A roar splits the sky

The chains that bind crumble,
Into dust the shackles melt away
A fully formed being,
From the bowels of the earth emerges
Eyes flaming bright red with curiosity
And the wonder of a baby
In fascination, the gentle behemoth,
Scans the terrain, marvelling

All eons past flash before his curious eyes
The past revealed
Enslavement, imperialism,
Colonialism and neo-colonialism
All tumble into view in their glory
And in their sordidness
The past is the past and cannot be undone
The future beckons

Where there was no foundation,
He resolves to establish,
A facade of magnificence
From the Earth's core soars
He takes a deep breath and a sigh
And the evils of the world flee
The barren earth bears fruit again
The droughts fade to antiquity
The world is made fecund
Where there was nothing, life springs

Runesu Chazvemba   Kemet Awakening

A Time of Glory

Under the desert sand, Kemet lies in repose
His visage, burnished brass in the sun, made
Here, the erstwhile glory of a million years past
Lies dormant in a mummified hibernation

Beneath the watchful eye of a myriad pyramids
Whose energies establish magnetic fields
A cocoon is soft and nurturing to sustain life
Sarcophagi carrying the treasures of eons past
The excavated tombs are repositories of decoys
Mummified remains are parodies of restoration

The true sarcophagi allows for hibernation
A hibernation to withstand a million years
Just as the uraeus is a symbol of eternity
The burnished brass-faced people are sovereign
Them who kindled the sun on earth
Those who built the pyramids, such as cosmic beacons

Their DNA, the vast plains of Africa, spread
The tongue of old in West Africa is vestigial
In the Bantu languages of the south, an echo
The sacred tongue endures all depredation
Just as beneath the pyramids, life unalloyed stirs
In the heavens, the constellations glide inexorably

When the clock of the universe aligns again

Runesu Chazvemba — Kemet Awakening

So, the cycle of life unfolds immaculately
The grand machines of old will roam the skies
To the universe, distant travel possibilities are vast
The stars whisper a melodious tune, for glory beckons!

Runesu Chazvemba   Kemet Awakening

A Glorious World

Khufu built the Great Pyramid gloriously
That sprawls upon the undulating sands
Of the Giza necropolis in its vastness.

The tincture of his skin,
By the unrelenting sun made,
Dark hued and baked as black could be
The whispers and sighs of black Africa
Across the continent and the world
Heard in their toil in the sun
To carve with their piercing intellect, unrelenting,
and a craftsmanship unparalleled in all history,
The Egyptian civilisation emerged
from the barren sand.

In every exertion and expedition of energy
The African brought forth life
From the swamps of the Nile
Life and a civilisation sprang
Our ancestors in one channelled, corroborative effort,
Mapungubwe from the savannah
Fashioned out of stone,
And Great Zimbabwe in the same light was built,
To be beacons and symbols of hope for ages to come,
we made the Zambezi River in a dream and a sigh
And the Congo River with our sighs and minds
Charged that the earth be cleaved and lie riven,

Runesu Chazvemba   Kemet Awakening

For the waters to liberally flow from hither to thither,
where the savannahs sprawl and thrive far and wide,
constructed from the cauldron of our minds.

Every tree that shoots off
Into the heavens with vigour,
And great purpose has our hand in its being,
We seeded the world with the most beautiful flowers
That here and there, and now bloom majestically
Beautifully, they bloom in our midst
Casting a sweet balm, of effulgence most sublime,
Sweet scented daffodils and lilacs.

We, in our sighs and murmurs in the wind, carved,
The world in valleys and mountains as we willed
We are builders of vast universes,
The artists for each aesthetic expression in nature
and the world, exhibited in flagrant abandon,
Of a texture and structure overflowing with beauty.

Runesu Chazvemba   Kemet Awakening

When doubt assails cock your head back,
And into the infinite cosmos unflinchingly stare,
For the grandeur above in all its astonishing beauty,
Is yours made with an unbridled flare of the ineffable,
That yet weaves a tapestry of magnificence,
In the fabric of the cosmos built an eternal jewel.
To bedazzle all generations to come with
beauty, Unequalled by anything ever in man's
dreams imagined.

Resolute and indomitable strength,
Carved in an aesthetic flair
A beauty without measurable depth,
A flowing and blossoming beauty,
An enduring testimony to an erstwhile glorious world
On the plain it lies unmoved
By the time it expires in the wind
But all the glory above revealed is but a mere iceberg,
The footprints of a time and glory
Gone beneath buried
Vast and expansive, it lies dormant,
Unseen in all its lustre.

But oh, it is there unblemished in all its splendour,
Ours is an immortal world imperishable in all ages,
only seen by those whose hands the ankh have wielded
a flaming torch in our hearts eternally lit!

Runesu Chazvemba   Kemet Awakening

The Eternal Land

A king in Benin
In a bronze statue
Magnificently immortalized
A pharaoh in ancient Kemet
In a gold-coated statue
A beauty unparalleled
An eternal beacon
An aesthetic flourish
Testimony to immaculate craftsmanship.
The denizens of this great land,
In a sigh fashioned.

Upon the Sudan sands
A myriad pyramids
Into the skies rise
Homing in on that place
In the skies, set
Star Sirius,
That eternal
abode.

Giant sculptures
Of beauty stands
Images of kings and queens
In marble, finely sculpted
Kings and queens resolute
Upon the encroaching sand,
Undaunted by the baking sun.

Runesu Chazvemba   Kemet Awakening

In Ethiopia
That famed land
Besought by the gods
The abode of the unsullied

The unconquered Kemet
Pristine unadulterated Kemet
Souls are pure and untouched
By the begrimed hands from other lands.

A temple in the sky rests
Oh, this enchanted land
Where Christianity bloomed
In these many millennia
past,
A civilisation long
A tradition enduring.

In Zimbabwe, the cairns of stone
On a savanna plain rises
The emperor's totem
In soapstone immortalised!

Runesu Chazvemba   Kemet Awakening

The death of intellect

I saw her lying by the roadside, mangled,
Limbs contorted into a fleshy swastika
With not a limb aligned in any one direction,
But each in its direction turned.

I knew her once; her name was intellect.
Now she lies dead, flesh mottled in grime
And yet her message lives on still
Undaunted by the desolating hand of death:
Should the same cobbled path our fathers trod,
We in our fresh feet also tread?

Stomping our toes on the same rock,
That stumped them,
Our flesh and blood to mingle
On a rock upon the path,
Don't you dream of the stars?
That lies beyond and above.

Don't you find the firmament fascinating?
In its twinkling glory, quite enticing?
Quite alluring to the senses,
Pleasing to that part of ourselves that is sentient.

Runesu Chazvemba — Kemet Awakening

Don't you wish for a world?
Without debilitating diseases?
A world without war, famine
Or any other human deprivations?
If the human mind has no limits
Except those that we put upon it;
wouldn't you want to stretch it?

To the uttermost that you possibly can
To experience life uninhibited,
Life to its fullest limit,
Unencumbered by anything?

She had moaned to a deafening silence
As she intoned to those who would listen
To all and sundry, she had preached
But now by the roadside she lies,
gone, smote by death, and flesh
expires
In broad daylight.

I am not all, she had said,
But through me, all is possible

Life in its fullest experience
Perceptions are unencumbered to expand
Ever and ever wider into the world
The firmament is not a limit but an infinite playground,
Where opponents roam in their multitudes
Filling the whole visible world
My limbs might melt and be swept away

Runesu Chazvemba — Kemet Awakening

In the midst of time flowing away
But I perish not for my imprints are everywhere.
In the sand, on the walls, on mountainsides
On tree barks gnarled by age, they cling,
In the sky, they hang to be read by all
I have seeded the world, and in each germination,
A new form springs forth to tell a story.

I'm the intellect moulder of all things,
Visible in the mundane world,
The builder of libraries, vast
The adept hand of the sculptor
That chisels out sculptures of great beauty and form
The autobahn or the highway is called.
The arching bridges and the spanning hanging bridges
The skyscrapers and the sprawling mansions,
The grand palaces of the old world and the new
The whirling houses in the sky,
The vessels to other planets go
All these I have fashioned
In their immortal wanderings,
Mine own immortality is guaranteed.

Kemet Awakening

Runesu Chazvemba

I slough off this mundane shell, heavy,
A wasting baggage with which I touched the world
But now in the charade of death,
The whole universe in my bosom I embrace
I'm intelligent, ignorance is my nemesis.
Each dusk, I die, and each dawn, I resurrect.
Mourn me not then, for I am the ever-winding coil,
The rainbow in each dew drop,
The vast, unending expanse of
space, in all its starry beauty,
unfurled,
A cosmic petal.

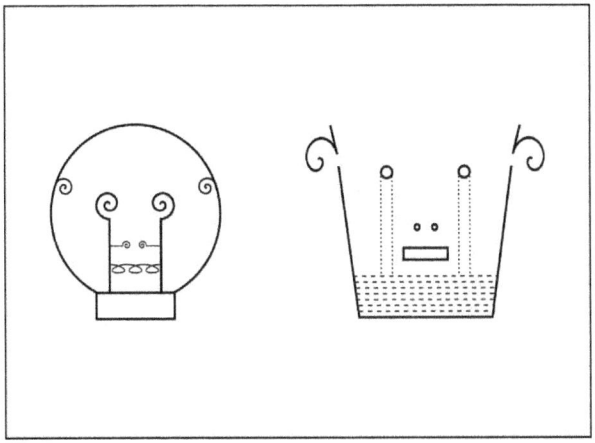

Enraptured dreams

Oh, there is a place of quiet
Far removed from the mundane world
A world of faulty senses is blind
Where the full perceptions of the world lie
Untainted by the grime of the flesh,
And a place of great tranquillity,
Of smooth flowing limbs that hover in the air.

The mind, oh, such a curious thing,
To all things beautiful and limitless drawn
To this place nightfall after nightfall,
When the night is heavy with sleep,
I journey floating into this ethereal
world, a wide world without
encumbrance.

I journey with confidence and excitement.
Amidst the placid, serene environments
To rest for a while and reflect upon life beneath
The whole land my bed make,
The earth and air around it,
Is the downy bed upon which I rest
With the star-spangled sky for a cushion
To spread around me and cover
I gently lay myself down to rest
To ponder in slumber the joy of dreams,
In a snore, the constellations in the
heavens are drawn in their various forms.

Runesu Chazvemba   Kemet Awakening

Oh, the other side of the moon
Pockmarked with meteor impact craters
A tranquil place of quiet,
A dark balm that wraps itself upon my being
Where sweet dreams eternal envelop and,
Flow soothingly upon the shrouded veins of the mind.

On the face of the moon, carved
Are the images of falling rain of the firmament?
In a blink, the whole universe blinks too,
Such a myriad starry twinkle.

On enraptured dreams,
An excursion into realms
Far removed from the daily tread
An opening of the portals of time and space,
To glance at the spectacular.

Flesh soft limbs ill-equipped,
For this enthralling journey
They are left in the depository of such encumbrances,
fashioned out of the mundane world of flesh,
Bone and dust that blow away in the wind.

Runesu Chazvemba — Kemet Awakening

The Earth in its whirling about its axis
A melodious tune whispers
A siren luring the unsuspecting sailors
In the universe, to swoop down and be merry
On enraptured dreams, a tapestry is fashioned,
Of immeasurable beauty
Fashioned from the shards of the mind!

The sepulchre forged from the illusory world
The sense dissolves
To display a rushing flood of escaping dreams
In a myriad shapes and forms
All this to regale the dreamer
With a brushing tingling sensation
That permeates the whole
Such sweet massaging
Of the fountain of existence
Proofed from ruin
Enraptured dreams of a whole world,
Of beauty and wonder, fashion.

Runesu Chazvemba   Kemet Awakening

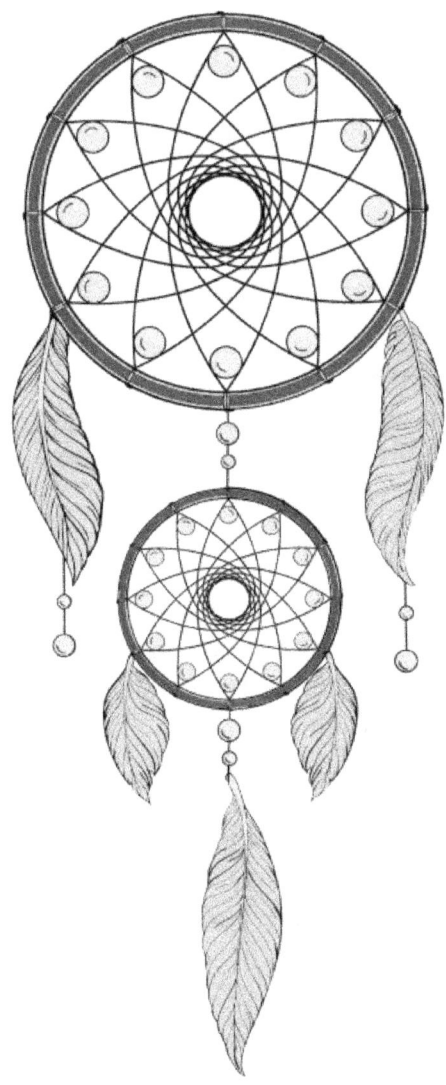

Runesu Chazvemba   Kemet Awakening

Unfurling Wings

There is naught here done.
Which, in earlier times, was not done by others
Great nations and men with force of arms
Lesser nations and men are subjugated
The plunder of wealth and dreams,
Oh, such a recurring motif in human
affairs.

The only armour against such excesses is,
For one to hitch oneself to a star
That from such lofty place no barb to reach,
By this act, one is set free from plunder
And from such a high place to contemplate
The vista of despair beneath the crawling clouds.

Oh, whimper not the tainting of a lily-livered mind
For it sure can shake itself clean
Mourn not the passing of the sun
For it is reborn with the dawn.
Plunder singes the flesh and crushes the bone
To a pulp, and the marrow oozes.

If on up high a pedestal of gold and other minerals
Then the tumbling is hard and long
Akin it is to the hurtling down of the meteor
Flaming and tail trailing, a snake in the sky
Blazing the sky crimson in a whirring,
A flaming streak, a brush of fire in the sky

Runesu Chazvemba   Kemet Awakening

The only armour against such tumbling is;
For one to hitch oneself to a star
That from such lofty place no barb to reach,
By this act, one is anchored, set free from
plunging and from such a high place to
contemplate the vista of despair beneath the
crawling clouds.

Oh, but fear not a crumbling demise
For the human vessel ought to withstand all
Unfurling wings, catch the wind from below
And halt the tumbling fury
On wings of the possible
And rejuvenating resolve
Soar to the heavens!

Unfurling wings,
Champion a new realm
Of glowing dreams
Of the future honeyed.
The horizon brightens
With the approaching glory of a new sunlit day.

Runesu Chazvemba   Kemet Awakening

The Impeccable Quarry

With a roar and whirring of the wings
The falcon glided through the thin air above
A thundering voice that reverberates.
Across the firmaments in a roaring fury intones.
Your crime announces the fiendish falcon;
'Is you have dared to soar on up high,'
It is a sacrilege in this kingdom
That you are so adept at a skill above your kind.
All these mottled souls in my bosom to keep,
Why challenge the immutable laws?

Be gone, oh, you with ingenuity
That seeps far and wide, the whole realm to cover
And pollute my kingdom with your penchant
For excellence in nature is found to be rare
This kingdom has no use for you
Sure, that I can attest, for the sky is not yours.
Cast be you to the ends of the world,
Where no eyes chance upon your antics.

Be gone like many of old who have dared
To snatch the fire from the crowns of the gods,
Never with your breath to tread upon this land,
For your feet profane the ground!

To Golgotha be gone to dangle in the barren valley.
Of an icy wind that cuts the flesh to ribbons
Vultures shall pursue and pare bones.
And the last shreds of you leave your bones bare.

Runesu Chazvemba — Kemet Awakening

With the flesh pared, the bones bared
The icy wind in time to polish the bones,
For the hyenas to gather and maul
In their frenzied hunger and acidic stomachs.

Before this elaborate fate expires
And restores the world to what it was before
Doves are to flutter to all corners of the world
In one fluttering flock of whitened wings,
To herald the gruesome demise of one,
Who dared to soar above your brethren?

Ravens to seed the earth with the news,
That from each seed an orchard to spread
You shall be appointed mad and feverish,
From a mania of unpronounceable terms.

Stones and thorns cast before you perish
To blow ashes in the speeding wind of time
I shall on this pedestal perch
To watch and relish your whimpering parting!
This immaculate struggle, and then you perish.
Beneath the shrouded wall of night.

Your weakness is your ingenuity,
In this land where mediocrity is all that counts
It is a sweet presence,
That ruffles everyone's feathers
and gives all a sweet slumber.

Runesu Chazvemba — Kemet Awakening

Your crime is that you are ingenious,
We have no use for such in this land
For this, be an impeccable quarry
And let the falcon tear you down
And seal your destiny.
Should your name be said?

It is forbidden!
For then it would announce to the world
That all is possible to all and sundry,
And the firmaments within reach
To outreaching hands!

Be gone, oh, you with ingenuity
That seeps far and wide, the whole realm to cover
And pollute my kingdom with your penchant
For excellence in nature is found to be rare
This kingdom has no use for you
Sure, that I can attest, for the sky is not yours.
Cast be you to the ends of the world,
Where no eyes chance upon your antics.

The impeccable quarry glides smoothly
Out of the approaching talons of the fiendish falcon
And in its roaring blast
The world with a gift of sight and flight is gifted!

Runesu Chazvemba   Kemet Awakening

The Immortal Wanderers

Earth is our home now,
But it has not always been our place of abode.
Oh, this world is shrouded in a misty cloud
The blue shows here and there
The dark sprinkled azure
Veiled from the prowling pirates of the universe.

It is only a child, a newly born world
In the vast universe of ancient worlds
For we are immortals, wanderers
Through the vast outer space in search of new worlds
When the universe is in labour
We offer ministrations
Upon the birth agonies of a new world
With our breath and intentions
On a barren world to imbue with the seeds of life.

Though in life, trapped it seems
In the world shrouded in a vast straitjacket,
fashioned out of flesh, blood, and bones
That ache and crumble in the fleeting reality.

In death, we are resurrected again,
Disabused of mortal trappings, immortal we rise
The birds of the sky in the mundane world we admire
Pale in comparison to our true selves
With the illusion of existence tossed in the abyss,
The true nature shows like a beacon in the dark.

Runesu Chazvemba — Kemet Awakening

In huge fluttering wings
We soar to the highest heavens
Where the air is thin and fresh
Far out and higher up than any bird
Of the feather that has ever flown,
We climb to the highest heaven
We pervade the world with our beauty
And the magic of being and our act in the
physical manifest to fashion a galaxy
Here and there with bursting lights
That of the azure in abandoned beauty is carved.

A beautiful image of the sky,
A streaking fiery brightness
That paints the domed canvas of heaven
In a dash of creativity overflowing
In the firmament, the Milky Way is drawn
With such a flourish of hand,
To mark a path of wandering spirits
In a cosmic play of universal proportions.

Earth is our home now,
But it has not always been our place of abode
Oh, this world is shrouded in a misty cloud
The blue shows here and there
The dark sprinkled azure,
Veiled from the prowling pirates of the universe.

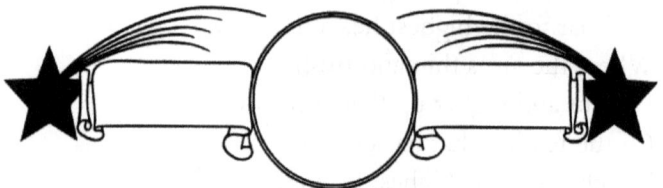

In Art Immortalised

Inexorably, time ticks on,
In its wake, glory is swept away,
Under the carpet of yesterday
From Antarctica to the Arctic,
Civilisations of grandeur once thrived;
Now under the ice and sand are buried,
Grub for juvenile worlds to kick about!

In Africa, the Giza Necropolis attests,
To the enduring culture of the ancients,
Now in the sand deeply buried.
The Americas' own pyramids,
Laid in an encroaching forest,
Thick and teeming with serpents
From America to Asia,
The world is riddled with these pyramids,
That foretells a time of glory.

Africa in the centre rests,
The cradle of humankind,
The fountain of life, where it all began.
This continent is the repository
Of all great civilisations,
The root of all that followed
At Giza, the pyramids of ancient times,
To this day, stand undaunted by time

Runesu Chazvemba — Kemet Awakening

A shimmering testimony of a glory interred,
Only partially interred
For the greater part isn't.

A civilisation of antiquity that has withstood,
The unrelenting assault of piling sands
Shifting sands, encroaching dunes,
Bent on burying expert pieces
Of art in architecture.

The pyramids stand,
From the earth-shattering quakes,
The orgiastic[1] tremors of the earth
The pyramids stand,
Unmoved by the rushing winds
Of the desert that blows maleficent

In Sudan, a myriad pyramids stand,
These are relics from the mighty Nubian civilisation.
In Antarctica, a pyramid crests
The frozen icy terrain,
To stake its claim to glory in architecture.

Oh, but Earth is one huge tomb,
That buries the crumbling bones of antiquity,
But in art lives on,
Art immortalises them all,
In sculptures,
Structures of beauty
And in rock paintings immortalised.

---

[1] Orgiastic: of or resembling an orgy.

Runesu Chazvemba — Kemet Awakening

The creative works of all ancient civilisations,
Do tell a tale of the great lives they led.
It is the aesthetic expression that blazes a trail,
For a life lived sumptuously[2], in art, captured
All that is visible and human-caused of varying
beauty And style mark the path of those before.

Inexorably, time ticks on,
In its wake, glory is swept away,
Under the carpet of yesterday
From Antarctica to the Arctic,
Civilisations of grandeur once thrived.
Now, under the ice, water and sand are buried,
Grub for juvenile worlds to kick about!

It is art, it is art that encapsulates it all,
And in a glowing vignette[3] display to regale the world.
Without art, all perishes and dissolves into dust
And is swept away in the amnesia of life.

Art, art immortalises it all, the beauty of today,
Into the future projected in its eternal glory
Ignorance unveiled, beneath its gnarled feet,
The proof of antiquity's glory lies buried
Awaiting that chancy encounter with a spade,
Wielded by an archaeologist bent on truth.
Eureka!

And the glory of old to the world made known.

---

[2] Sumptuous: splendid and expensive looking.
[3] Vignette: a picture that shades off gradually into the surrounding paper.

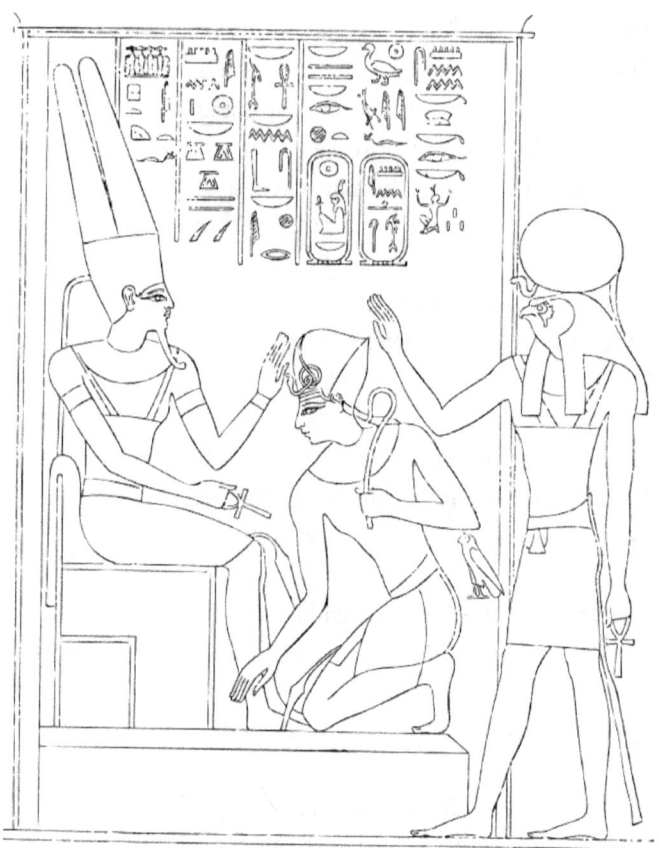

Ignorance Unveiled

Oh, the veil of ignorance
Does casts a pale pall across the mind,
All the greatness and what is good
And possible in the world,
The amorphous[4] cloak of the unknown
From searching eyes hide
Beneath the surface of the slimy, greasy pool,
Fishes of beauty lurk.

Oh, only inches from the cranial pate,
The seat of consciousness resides
The veil of ignorance conceals a snare
To ensnare man in its talons thick
The beauty in the world in all its flowery glory
From the eyes hid.

Hope such a bright flare in the dark,
To illuminate the path ahead,
A huge swathe upon the wide plains
of a vast grassland.

There to be seen by those with eyes
Attuned[5] to this marvel unfolding
With the mental and spiritual stamina
To withstand a marvellous scene.

---

[4] Amorphous: without clearly defined form or shape.
[5] Attuned: made receptive or aware.

Runesu Chazvemba — Kemet Awakening

Sinuous swelling energy gracefully
Flowing without cessation, A
whirl, a dance, all-encompassing,
Devouring of the senses flared.
The poet rests not until the veil
Ignorance has been lifted off.

To shine a luminous glow,
Upon the all-encompassing shadow of ignorance,
The light of truth as gleaned
From the observable universe
Fights back in incensed fury,
Rises to cast the veil of ignorance off
and light shines through.

Ignorance in a crumbling heap of greyed shadows
Escapes into the void.
Defeated resoundingly for now, so it seems
But beneath seething, venomous!
Waiting for an opportune moment
To spring forth and smite
Reducing all that is precious
And treasured to a smouldering pile.

Runesu Chazvemba — Kemet Awakening

Wisdom shining piercingly
Bores deeply into the muck,
Screeching ignorance unveiled.
And the world becomes a better place, is born,
To cower no more beneath the gooey slime
Of unreasoning fear
Those claws with long talons
And sharp and greyed with dirt!

Runesu Chazvemba   Kemet Awakening

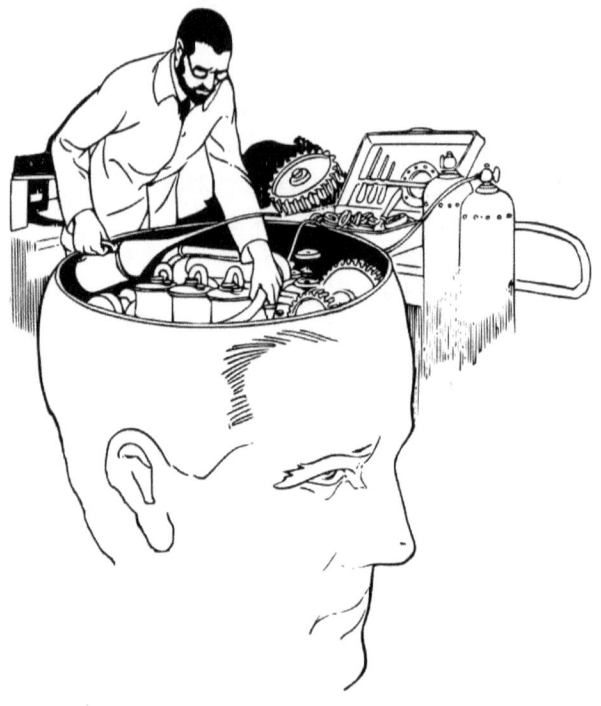

In Kemet

In times gone dreams abounded
The reaches of Kemet had no bounds
On land, sea, and the skies
The African people conquered
The distant stars were upon their gaze
They measured the constellations
They are a land-travelling,
Seafaring and spacefaring lot
Weapons of astounding power, they had
They were experts in the physical world

They who plumbed the depths of the human soul.
God-fearing and God knowing.
The arcane nature of the human soul
Upon the stele, in a hieroglyphic flourish drawn
And on papyrus written to be
read,
Oh, this ancient text lays bare
The secrets of antiquity.

All that existed and was known
Vestiges of these in our African DNA exist
To be activated by those who deign to be!

Runesu Chazvemba   Kemet Awakening

Chapter Two
Poems of Resolve

Conquer thyself. Till thou hast done this, thou art but a slave for it is almost as well to be subjected to another's appetite as to thine own.

-Robert Burton (1577- 1640) *Anatomy of Melancholy*

The Sentry

On his feet, he stands
Steady as steady could be
From dawn to dusk, unwavering
And undaunted, he stands.

Vigilant and rapt[6] he stands.
Oblivious to the lack of comforts
The sentry he is forfeits.
The comforts of rest on soft cushions.

Scanning the horizon for a flicker of motion
For a gleam of light,
He stands high up on a pedestal
Of his own lanky feet that support him on high
With eyes as sharp as those of a hawk,
Flickering and scanning the world beneath,
Observing all and missing nothing
Beneath the vista of life unfolding.

Upright he stands stiff as a rod
He stands, unmoved by the unravelling drama
Wind swept and pummelled,
By the unrelenting wind of passing days
Scorched in the merciless burning heat

---

[6] Rapt: completely fascinated or absorbed by what one is seeing or hearing.

Runesu Chazvemba — Kemet Awakening

Of a calloused[7] Sun that sends flames hot
To singe off the flesh of solid rock,
In the mould of a human-made.

Birds of a multiple variety perch
On his pate to preen and chirp,
Oblivious to where they perch
With their drooping shoulders besmeared[8]
Mottled in droppings, he stands.

His gaze unwavering, staring unblinking,
Scanning the horizon in unblinking eyes,
Eyes that see everything and miss nothing
In the lands beneath the plinth,

To the ocean that stretches beyond the horizon
At night, his flaming eyes scan the seas
A beacon for seafaring vessels to a place to moor
A promise of hope beyond the watery tomb,
To a drowning sailor, hands in plea and supplication[10]
The sentry unmoved stands
Undaunted by the tumult of the sea
And the maelstrom of land in agitation.

---

[7] Calloused: feeling or showing no sympathy for others.
[8] Besmeared: smear or cover with a greasy or sticky substance.
[10] Supplication: the action of asking or begging for something earnestly or humbly.

Runesu Chazvemba   Kemet Awakening

Runesu Chazvemba   Kemet Awakening

Ambition Burnt

Without overweening ambition
To stretch out the wings
And let fly to the skies,
Is life not but a dross?

A drudgery that draws out the day,
To stretch indefinitely?

Whenever a great ambition swamps,
Let it seize and to the heavens soar,
It could be a reminder to one of Icarus
Tumbling, but let it be a hollow ring
The fear that such thoughts evoke
Might let all one's ambition surge and subside
For there is no greater terror,
Than the hurtling down
To a crumbling heap of flesh and blood!

Oh, the horror of such a plummeting,
Fills the heart with dread.
To one's demise one hurtles,
With no brakes to stop the streaking inferno
And all ambition crashed to a bonfire
Of huge lapping flames
That towers to the heavens.

Runesu Chazvemba — Kemet Awakening

To blood and gore,
The dreams and ambition
Turned red with
disappointment.
Oh, burning ambition
Though it paints the skies with
passion,
It is all but short-lived.

May your flame then be brief?
And inconspicuous[9]
To be shrouded from the starry gaze,
Be extinguished forthwith.
Before the eyes of the world have glimpsed upon you
And save you from ignominy[10],
Of a hurtling streak across the dome of heaven,
But if you amount to anything,
Let it be in the subterranean[11] world,
With no eyes to stare,
That in your rising, you do so fully-
formed
And ready to show the world,
That which it cannot destroy.

Burnt ambition smouldering embers,
Burn with a fury unspent and now uncoiling.

---

[9] Inconspicuous: not clearly visible or attracting attention.
[10] Ignominy: public shame or disgrace.
[11] Subterranean: existing, occurring, or done under the earth's surface.

Runesu Chazvemba   Kemet Awakening

Ambition is made of imperishable stuff
From the lapping flames of the pyre,
That the uncertainties of life hurl
Dare we rise, reaching ever for that goal!

Runesu Chazvemba   Kemet Awakening

Solitude

O solitude, solitude!
Thou art a splendid state
To be experienced in full,
From the depth of solitude
A great growl issued forth and,
A great many things sprang
To full view in the glare of daylight
Christianity in solitude
Of the wilderness was spawned;
The messiah went wandering, In
the wilderness in solitude.

In solitude,
The seeds of monastic religion were sown.
Prayer in the solitude of the mind
It is conducted each in solitude.
Islam in solitude
Of the prophet's stay in the cave was forged.
Buddhism under the solitude of the Boa tree,
Sprouted from the Buddha's brow.

Runesu Chazvemba — Kemet Awakening

Oh, it is solitude, solitude
From which great many things spring.
The chant and whirling din of the great multitudes,
The mind addles.
In the solitude of a dream
The mind bathes itself and rises cleansed.
Each particular is unique,
And from that kernel[12] of uniqueness.
Hope springs eternally
And a bright world is fashioned.

Oh, solitude, the bairn[13] of many,
A great deed into the world revealed,
The foundry upon whose forge
A great many artefacts are fashioned.
The cradle and natural habitat
Of the human individual spirit.
Drifting eternally through
The infinite vastness of the universe,
Dauntless in solitude,
Resolute in the drifting winds of the cosmos.

Ah, solitude, a cocoon so expansive
Of comforting white softness
That cleaves to the heart
With such a caressing, soothing warmth!

---

[12] Kernel: the central or most important part of something.

[13] Bairn: a child.

Runesu Chazvemba   Kemet Awakening

Indigence of the Soul

Oh, of all wretchedness of the human condition,
None rivals the indigence of the soul.
The vilest of man's scourges;
Is the indigence of the soul,
Pauperism assails, and the soul wears a cowl.
Slinks furtively from cove to cove
In the thick of the night,
With nothing but shadows in pursuit.

An eminent, glowing ball of life
With a potential unlimited,
Contorted into the grotesque of matter!
Like all lumps of flesh and blood,
Dependent upon other entities for sustenance.
This cleaver of universes and creator of life!
Labouring under the false impression of the created.
Knobby and gnawed hands outstretched for alms,
Seeking the license from other beings to survive.

Oh, this indigence of the soul is rank!
Eschew, therefore, any immersion into dirtied waters,
Let loose the girdle of the mind
And let your soul soar,
That it may be set free from the indigence of the soul,
Oh, indigence is not the native state of the soul!

Runesu Chazvemba   Kemet Awakening

Rise above the dirtied hands of indigence!
Slough off the constricting confines of indigence.
Soar to the heavens and let rot the indigence.
Rise, rise high and sink not into a muddied pond
Whose depths are infinite and crawling with grotesque
Creatures, heavy and bloated with venom,
Slithering monstrous creatures full of slime!

Runesu Chazvemba   Kemet Awakening

Emptiness

Karnak with her sheep-headed sphinx sentries,
In the distance looms a beckoning all with her allure,
Come hither, it seems to say in a droning whisper,
That echoes across the vast, barren desert
terrain.
The sand-laden wind moans in sympathy,
We are all in this together,
It seems to say.

Inside the temple of Karnak, vast are its spaces,
Infinite space, yet so empty.
Deserted and forlorn, a look it bestows
Upon any who dare visit this empty immensity.

Where art thou, worshipers, is an echo,
That reverberates through its halls at footfalls.
Silence enfolds the caverns of Karnak,
But if you close your eyes and let your mind swim,
filling the vast spaces with your unbridled self,
Oh, the stories it tells are numerous and exciting.
A ritualized dance of the soul in the heavens reflected
A mind unwinding to fill the heavens with gold
particles of delight and promise of life
Enchanted in the starry sky.

Runesu Chazvemba — Kemet Awakening

Oh, take me to Karnak that my soul may
soar,
Unbridled to fill the ever-expanding universe.
To dance amidst the echoing emptiness,
That I may sing songs to Orion and Sirius.
That the old glory of those forlorn enchanted times
might in the fullness of time from the desert emerge?
Resplendent in the golden cloak of that era,
faded,
Buried in the vast sand
Of the ever-encroaching dunes.

Oh, take me to Karnak where the sages of old trod,
That in the sand where footprints lay buried,
I prod
To reveal the glory of old,
And restore Karnak to its erstwhile glory!
A dollop of beauty in the sand etched.
Reflecting the beauty of the heavens above,
The constellations that straddle the heavenly dome, A mirror of the ineffable in stone carved.

Runesu Chazvemba   Kemet Awakening

Oh, take me to Karnak where the spirit takes form,
take me to that famed sacred land the gods trod.
Uplift my spirit and let my mind soar to the
sky,
To bask in the vast expanse of space, A realm
without boundaries.
A full emptiness.

Oh, take me to Karnak, that abode of the gods.
Who in ancient times on earth trod.
Sacred is the land of Karnak.
A spiritual abode, a doorway to eternity!

Runesu Chazvemba   Kemet Awakening

Runesu Chazvemba   Kemet Awakening

A Lament of the Ancient

Oh, my veins, all these millennia
Are filled with the fire of the mind,
My passions run deep
As the infinite pool of the spirit.
Oh, my heart pulses with the force and fury of the sun.
My mind is still bright and filled with infinite dreams.

Wholesome dreams on fertile ground are
planted, with sunrise leaves lush and full to
sprout.

Oh, these seeded nuggets, most precious,
With a trembling hand, knobby and gnawed,
I reach out and touch and caress with tenderness.

The ancient laments throughout the ages,
Hewing to a time encapsulated for all times to stay
Untarnished by the shifting wind of time expiring.
Resolutely set in form imperishable.
For it is not all depredation[14] on choice predicated?

I have bathed in the enchanted pool,

---

[14] Depredation: plundering or an act of attacking.

Runesu Chazvemba — Kemet Awakening

That bestows life unending upon the bather.
I have swum in the depths of an infinite pool,
Where fish blow kisses at you in playfulness,
And the bubbles that so issue out fill the depths
With unending reflections of the deep.

With limbs supple, I contort like a coiled spring,
Unwinding to stretch out for the clouds above,
Landing effortlessly and stretching out again
Ah, youth eternal, a cascading flow of life.

A Metamorphosis

What does it matter as to what universe?
What does it matter whether one
Is a master or a commoner drifting aimlessly?
That man wields power over others,
Or cringes under the power wielded by
others.

What burden must one's puny shoulders carry?
What load must be piled up on his crumbling back?
Must man heave heavy loads at every turn?
For what?
For whom must all these be conducted?

I am, without question, I'm so all is in me.
Universes blow at the slightest provocation.
Universes are born from nothing in the void.
Oh, they blow without regard to anything or anyone.
What does it matter whether one is clothed or not?
What importance does it all have to anyone?
But please do tell without any mincing of the words,
Who amongst men, in his multitude and environment,
Has not in mud crawled, on a soft belly tender?

We humans, frail humans trudging through life,
We hang by a flimsy tendril, gossamer thin.
Ah, but with such tenacity we cling, but why cling?
To that which perishes,

Runesu Chazvemba   Kemet Awakening

And is blown away in the wind of time?
Yet in our true nature
We are self-sustaining and indomitable,
Carrying on inexorably from eon to eon
Through spaces vast!

Each universe is a blink in the cosmos
Twinkling in the distance
Bright and glowing at our approaching
And fading into nothing,
At our parting, and recession
From one world into the other,
Surrender is the chant,
A riveting refrain from eon to eon,
Borne on the wind of time, vanishing,
And reforming again.
To melt and reform with a sickening repetition
Of a time-worn dance,
That clings to the back of the mind,
Taunting one with sound,
An eerie sound of ancient times,
Caught in amber of energy electric.

Seized in the relentless jaws
Of a rabid monster of the galaxy,
From which the chance of escape is remote,
Surrender then,
Let it all slip through your mental
And emotional terrain,
And surrender to that which is all-conquering
And monstrous,
That in the void of surrender
You may rise again to soar to the heavens,

Runesu Chazvemba — Kemet Awakening

Free and unhinged
From that which holds in the muck.

Unencumbered by anything mundane
But free from all yokes and chains,
Is the natural preserve of the human.
A thing to be surrendered?
Ah, but if surrender means a life
Divested of strive and toil,
Then surrender that the birthright
Over all creatures be restored,
Let the surrender be,
A dignified one apparelled in decorum,
Not a finality of a white flag hoisted,
And letting the gauntlet down
Routed by an enemy superior.

This is a metamorphosis,
A coming into being of something other,
For the new to rise from the old ashes
A surrender is called upon.
The new cannot spring forth
From the decaying form of the old,
Surrender and let the new come forth
Bright and resplendent,
Apparelled in the regalia of a new being!

Runesu Chazvemba   Kemet Awakening

Runesu Chazvemba   Kemet Awakening

The Black Prometheus

With arms stretched high
Lifting up a trident flaming red,
Hot from the furnace of the mind
That fanned it to a red glow,
Rose Prometheus resolute
And determined he rose,
With an ire befitting a god at the slight of men.

In the eye of the sleeping god, thrust deeper to sear,
The sinews of the mind
Flayed and cast out in a vortex.
The god in awakening indignation filled,
Poured out a torrent of wrath,
In a tidal wave of rolling fury,
He rises, and Prometheus is smitten.

Barren is the land upon which he stood,
Yet in every whisper and bosom
Of any living soul, the name Prometheus
Lies etched and riven in the very fabric of it.

It is the story of the mortal arching forth
Stretching out to embrace immortality,
That lies buried
Beneath a false facade of the mundane. The
world of flesh and blood and sedated senses,
Blinded to the ethereal beauty that abounds.
Prometheus set the flame of life aglow,
In the sky, it burns bright a beacon to others,

Runesu Chazvemba   Kemet Awakening

To home in on that immortal abode of the gods, an erstwhile haven for gods alone, but no more!

Runesu Chazvemba   Kemet Awakening

Ruins

Here it lies scattered in the dishabille of stones
Of all shapes and hues and sizes.
Rocks on the vlei scattered off-handedly,
An act of art and a prey to wantonness
A citadel of great magnificence,
A thought-out structure once stood.
In times past, it bespoke of a golden embroider,
A glory that was a marvel to the world.

In ruins now it lies, bearing no resemblance,
To the jewel it once was in times gone.
Ravaged by time, the elements and,
The overweening avarice of men
For things of beauty
From far and wide, they came and,
Pillaged her of her gold-encased jewellery
and ivory finery.

Soapstone sculptures of nature in their beauty,
And priceless to realms beyond carted in truckloads!
All her granite hewed vaults, by dynamite blasted,
and emptied of their treasures.
Her inner sanctum, pure self, violated,
Laid bare to the slimy hands of treasure
hunters.

Runesu Chazvemba   Kemet Awakening

The treasures to whom it was the depository,
Whisked off in the shroud of night to lands afar
There, to be presented as souvenirs,
Worthy of sovereigns
Of other thrones in palaces beyond.
All this under the watchful eye of the bateleur eagle,
A sky god who rides the wind from up high.

The Conical Tower whispered
To have borne the Eye of Horus,
In antiquity, the sky god motif was again etched.
A peregrine falcon symbolized,
The ultimate protector,
From above the Giza
Necropolis, it soared, seeing all
beneath.

Oh, as above, it is below,
As in the north, it is in the south,
One land, one people, all humanity, a medley of voices.

Eight birds from soapstone are sculpted,
And on pedestals set,
To gaze and protect those beneath the stars.
These are from the cairns of monoliths pulled down
And carted away to lands distant and alien,

With this, the spirit of the land
Snatched to lands beyond.
Oh, but time, patient time,
The bateleur eagle's wings stretched
From distant lands comes back home to roost.

Runesu Chazvemba — Kemet Awakening

These gods of the sky have come back home again,
What history and misfortune have laid to ruin,
In our resolve, cairn upon cairn we build again,
And a façade of magnificence takes shape on the vlei.

Skyscraper with chevron designs
And images of a bateleur eagle.
The Zimbabwe Bird, its portals adorn.
The Eye of Horus from the sky scans and,
A jewel in the sand beneath takes form.

A civilization in the making rises,
The grandeur of the heavens above,
Below is reflected.
The starry sky on the ground was drawn with a flourish,
An imitation of the expansiveness
Of the heavens above.
What was in time gone will be again established.
On this sacred ground heaven made.

Runesu Chazvemba   Kemet Awakening

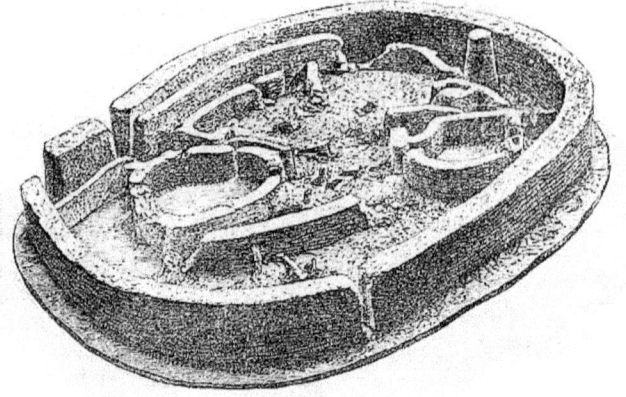

Runesu Chazvemba   Kemet Awakening

In Search of Glory

We have hopped from galaxy to galaxy,
On our spirit-propelled vessel
Self-made and generated,
Driven by a force from within,
We have voyaged across the
cosmos, we have.

On planets barren and covered in nothing,
But a scraggy rock have lived;
To world is covered from corner to corner in water
We have journeyed thereupon established worlds,
Others are filled with lush forests,
A flourishing flora and fauna we saw
Systems with several planets,
Habitable and teeming with human life,
Of valleys that cleave deep into the ground
And green with vegetation lush, Of
satellites numerous whirling
Over and over, above lights in the
sky.

Technologies unimaginable in our time
We have seen displayed,
From these we have borrowed
To build our own for the time to
come.

Runesu Chazvemba — Kemet Awakening

When we find that one patch of ground firm,
Lush with vegetation
Teeming with life, we can live side by side,
Without fear of being devoured.

 Oh, Earth, we chanced upon you
In our travels,
And so, enticing were you.
Your very depths oozed with gold
and other precious minerals.
All we had to do was take form again
And scoop and mould this malleable metal,
Gadgets of beauty and use we fashioned
And a civilization of gold began.
For glory we did, for glory we maintained it,
for generations to come.

Every ounce of adventure
Was this fine point conceived
And when all is told, it was glory,
It was glory that spurred us on to great deeds.

Runesu Chazvemba   Kemet Awakening

Renewal

Do not mourn the falling leaf.
Do not mourn the leaf that has fallen,
Its seeming death is not in vain.
From a leaf, ground union life grows.
Do not mourn the falling leaf,
To earth it descends to give life.
Do not mourn the fallen leaf,
For it brings life in its decomposition.
Celebrate it then and know that it brings life.
In doing this in it is resurrected.

Do not mourn the falling leaf,
Every fallen leaf brings renewal.
Mourn not that which transforms
Into something else.
Do not mourn the passing away of the material,
For life is eternal from each material death
It is resurrected and brought back to life.

Shed no tear drop for a falling rain drop,
In its muffled whistle as it plummets down
From the lofty heavens above, drawn to earth.

Runesu Chazvemba — Kemet Awakening

Shed not a tear for a plummeting raindrop
For it falls into the love embrace of earth,
Whose womb nurtures it before its ascendancy
At the behest of his majesty, the glowing disk
That glides the heavens, its crown resplendent.

Do not shed a tear for the falling raindrop
For its existence is eternal waxing and waning
Forever changing form from invisible to visible
An unending cycle of disappearance and appearance
Ascendance, coalescence, and a plummet to the
earth, A spluttering embrace with the earth,
An eternal dance between heaven and earth!

Runesu Chazvemba   Kemet Awakening

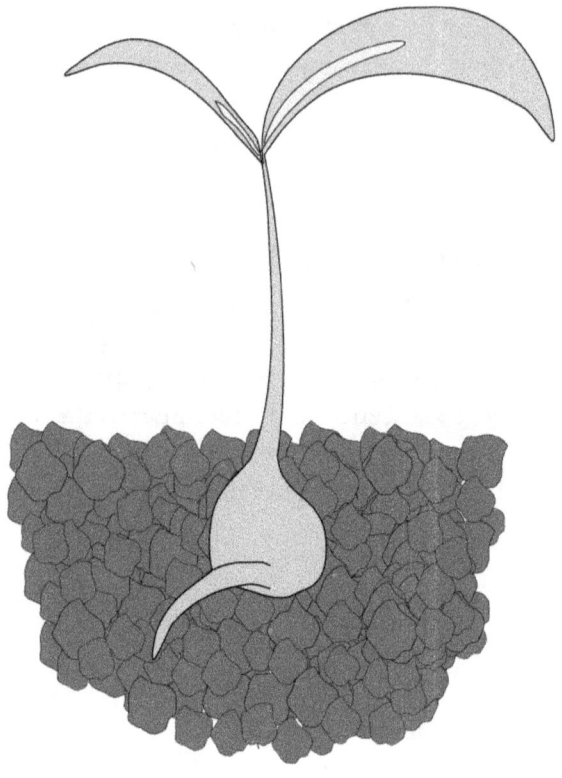

Chapter Three
Universe of the Mind

I have reared a monument more enduring than bronze and loftier than the royal pyramids, one that no wasting rain, no unavailing north wind can destroy; no, not even the unending years nor the flight of time itself. I shall not wholly die. The greater part of me shall escape oblivion.

-Horace (65- 8 B.C.) *Odes*

All a Dream

All sweet dreaming
To naught come
'Tis all but a shadow
Etched deep on the wall
Yet all so quicksilver
Fleeting is this bright shadow
Frail and gossamer thin
To slip through the fingers
Like sand through a sieve
And is gone?

Nay, it is all mirrors
A thin line divides the shadows
From the solid reality.

The fluid nature of dreams
Nature in its form recreates

All is sweet dreaming
The solid world firm
Was but a dream once,
Dream at will then!

Runesu Chazvemba   Kemet Awakening

A Mirror Reflection

Each turn, each twist a torment,
Oh, rueful, rueful dance,
A dervish driven green with envy.
With each intoxicating moment
An immersion into the fetid cesspool.
Is it possible for the heart to corrode?
While it pulses within the breast?

Oh, ignoble bent an albatross upon the neck,
Leaded soul that sinks into the murky earth, A
heavy heart wearied beyond ennui.
Each tread a flecking off of the rind upon the being.

Ah, this endless, tangled ordeal,
Who wove such a cunning snare?
A craft so flawless, the gods might despair,
Yet spun by my own hand, a fate self-made.
Oh, fury drives me toward a goal of my own design,
Self-propelled to glory's door,
Only to hang, the hangman, mine.

Runesu Chazvemba   Kemet Awakening

Upon the Crucifix

Oh, how could one have been blind?
To an imperilled integrity?
When all the tell-tale signs of its attrition,
Abounded in everything that was on display.
The fading glances, fleeting shadows
The eyes that couldn't look one in the eye,
But now, crucified integrity on the cross
dangles, Carrion for vultures in the sun dries.

In those places in shadow, maggots sprout,
Ugly, fat, and hairy on festering flesh feed.
Ah, the stench, a thick pall of putrefaction,
Repulsive in a sweeping cloud about one.

The skies darkened at night,
Day in shadow, overcast,
Light through the fissures
escapes,
Life once taken flight is gone!

The mundane part of life expires
The spiritual side is imperishable
It is this that must be safeguarded
From the torture through association with the bodily,
Upon the crucifix of life!

Runesu Chazvemba — Kemet Awakening

Upon a Pawn

Upon a pawn, peace is predicated.
This vassal, a vessel once prized,
A soul in pawn held for posterity,
That this vessel is for safekeeping
It is not to be dented and tossed
Upon the waters shallow
To shatter at the shoals
That awaits beneath.

Treasure this vassal, sure
Of great use it is that I know
Tossed it not to the winds
And let no vulture and other carrion mangle
This vehicle, upon which many great things hinge
Treasure it and keep it safe from the elements

Runesu Chazvemba   Kemet Awakening

Crude Sculpture

A grotesque sculpture
A piece of red-hot iron
Flattened on a dented anvil
By a faltering hand of a moronic silversmith
An ink blot sank deep
Into the core of a valuable book
The unheard, the unfelt glow of a distant star
The tentative and subtle
Thumping, eerie sound in the night
Of the heartbeat of an unborn child!

A turd coalescing with other turds
To form a lump of excreta,
Bobbing up and down
The common sewer waters of a decaying society.
The scream that dies down at one's throat,
The blank stare of an imbecile
The inequality of all creatures under the sun. The
distant, ominous drone of an approaching
Armageddon!
The annihilation of yesterday,
Looking back on tomorrow.
Pigsty a consciousness, the groan of a putrefying soul.
Purgatory beckons: hell is an ultimate destiny.
Oh, but heavenly beings triumph!

Runesu Chazvemba   Kemet Awakening

Superstitious Murmurs

The mystic significance of a meowing cat
The eeriness imbued in the hooting of an owl
The superstitious feel evoked,
By the drawn-out howling of the dogs in the night,
A tragedy imbued in the unknown.

Marionette dangles and jiggles
To the adept pulling of strings
The stench of burnt integrity
Instead of people,
There stands a taxidermist collection!

An ancient chant of the never would be
A repose in the crypt of time
The mind is a nemesis
Rectitude a curse
Purity a weakness
The undug-up jewel in the grub rots!

Receding Glory

Evanescent memories into shadows retreated
Beautiful, gilded memories faded
Precious nuggets of an existence forgotten,
Fading, receding traces of glory
In its place, what's left?
Nothing but a yawning chasm,
Dark and bottomless.

Such is the nature of life in the gloomy shadows
Of a fretful heart whose caverns are bereft of light
Light does not only come from the sun
For the greatest light rests within
The torch from which it comes
Is lit by one's mental source

Hitch to that ester while glory
Recession, which is illusory,
Glory rest eternal
At the human breast.

The Dark Rider

Hail the gentleman with the scythe
On horse, dark he rides
He is tasked to expunge
To slumber and quietude
That is not a whisper heard
That all secrets lay hid
From prying human minds and eyes.

Oh, but dark ignorance
Can the brightness of a starlit night be hidden?
Can the vastness of space
Behind a finger be concealed?
The grave, such a ghastly tomb
Interment a lid heavy with concrete
Can the brightness of the sun from the gaze be hidden?

The Profligates

Profane ways of the profligate
Divested of apparel in corridors run amok
Staggering drunkenly through the alleyways
Those of loose virtues with skirts heaved
Catching the wind in places no wind should go.

Rank, rank is the breath
And the scent of putrefaction!

Runesu Chazvemba   Kemet Awakening

Thought Pollution

Born with a blank slate
Yet the imprint of the world
On the crown jewel that glitters
Lies are buried within the thin scalp
Shielded by an electric field that surrounds
But oh, not so immune to the mental pollution
That drifts in from other minds leprous.

The mind is a genesis oasis
The birthplace of creation and destruction,
All beauty and all ugliness spawned.

Dirge of the Ancients

To the Duat, to the Duat!
To the Duat, we must return
When our lives' journeys' ceased,
Oh, this sweet, glorious going
To a blissful place forever
glowing.

When all effort is expended
And all that remains is being
The Duat is the repository of the free
Like a magnet draws one into itself
When one's labours are done
And all toiling ceased,
Into bliss' embrace one falls.

The Gift of Sight

A kaleidoscope view of the world in bloom
The luminous clouds that scud across the sky
The magnificence of light
On different surfaces reflected
Green, blue, and yellow all fused
And many colours to make
Light to pierce through
The veil of things and reveal all,
A beauty of things and forms to see.

Runesu Chazvemba   Kemet Awakening

Tortured Pain

On the sofa, a giant lies
Groaning in pain
Frothing at the mouth,
White foam gathers.

Tortured pain,
Searing pain,
Red-hot fire blazes
Through the lining of the membrane
Of the brain.

Expiring in torment,
A ratchet breath issues out,
Searing heat, a soaring
pain.

The stench of death
Gathers about the room,
Walls creak in sympathy
Night gathers outside
Ready always to inundate and
fill the heart with dread!

Runesu Chazvemba   Kemet Awakening

The Red World

Grandeur strides across the celestial dome
Flaming red in angst and fury unspent, it rides
That ancient world of fire and brimstone
The gong that set the universe into a war frenzy
unleashed weapons of great devastation,
Of a power and fury worse than atomic bombs!

Now stripped of all fury and power overt,
it glides through the vastness
Of space in mock supplication.
Hidden within its bowels is a volatility unspent
A force of unimaginable proportions lies in wait
This erstwhile throne of the universe will rise again.
All appearances of desolation and wreckage of rocks
It is but a deception most sublime.

The red world Mars glides,
The red glowing throne of the universe
A hibernating force to be reckoned with
In slumber, it glides across the celestial dome.
A dead world, it appears, but life never left.

Runesu Chazvemba   Kemet Awakening

The Brightest Star

To stretch out one's arms and reach out
For the brightest of stars in the firmament
Unencumbered to reach out and snatch
The brightest of stars and to one's bosom bring!

Oh, brightest of the firmament star
Your essence and mine merged as one
Forged together in an ethereal bond
In the universe, we glide cheerily
With not a shred of care in the world
Brightest star, a jewel of mine
The night sky is set aglow in your brilliance

Oh, brightest star in the sky,
The redeemer in a dark, moonless
night,

The beacon to a home in the sky.

Runesu Chazvemba   Kemet Awakening

Runesu Chazvemba   Kemet Awakening

Draw the Curtains

Draw the curtains wide
And let the light flow in
The evening gentle light
All light, even the light of night,
To come in and bask
The room in its glow.

Oh, draw the curtains out
And let the light through
That sombre night
With its malevolent shadows
In the corner, cowed to hide
From the light of heaven,
That gentle breeze
A cool night floods through.

Runesu Chazvemba   Kemet Awakening

Writers Block

There is a deep well within
That bubbles and bubbles with poetry
Only the fountain from which heaven sends
It is clogged, clogged with the scourge, writer's block.
So, in infancy, ere ever the light of day was seen,
A stillbirth has become lost to the world.

Shall it be mourned?
Will there be a wail? But
who mourns and wails, for
what was never seen?
For what was never born? All
that could be lies buried
Beneath the heavy cloak.

What conquers this scourge?
Oh, it is the inspiring vastness of the sky,
The unending expanse of a starry sky,
A spring that gushes eternally!

Runesu Chazvemba   Kemet Awakening

Conversations with Judas

I seized him with the scruff of his mind
And shook him in fury
Tell me, Judas, tell in all honesty, do tell all
Before I fling you to the fringes of existence,
What compelled you to indulge in such a heinous act?
Full of rank, of perfidy?

To take a soul so pure and glowing
With the seed of immortality and hope,
To dash the fragile vessel of the immaculate one
onto the craggy hill of expedience!
Lured by the glittering metal
Of no more than thirty pieces,
Silver, it is called.

A friend and a master of the slimy hands
Of greedy and covetous men delivered!
Judas stares back through his fiery red eyes
Of a mind with a guilt deep and forbidding.
Two millennia of trod
Upon the earth, I have endured
Laden by the cloak of shame, heavy,

Runesu Chazvemba — Kemet Awakening

Haunted by visions of own perfidious heart,
Pursued by the shadows of their dark avarice
Life after life without cessation,
With no cowl of the mind
Dark enough to hide behind
I have sought chastisement for that deed, horrible,
from the hands of all would-be executioners.

For millennia of torture, I have endured.
The burning ashes of Pompeii baked me,
Through Genghis Khan's Cruelty
And a mountain of human skulls and rivers of blood.
A sojourn in Europe's blood baths,
Of the First and Second World Wars,
Full of the stench of gas chambers!

Here I stand, he moaned, with no reproof,
With no catharsis
For the DNA of my soul is eternally corrupted!

The Modern Cave

With a swoosh, the door to the lair opens
Jarred, it stands revealing the entrails
Of the cavernous space.

Flat and straight up are the walls of this cave
Against the wall of this cave, two-tier bunk beds rest.
In this portal, immaculately, we ingress
And are enclosed within the six walls.

Each bunk bed is to take and make a patch out of
White are the walls and a transparent portal
Reveals the world outside.
Up the ceiling of the cave
A luminescent light glows to shed light on
Shadows under the beds cower,
And when the lights are snuffed to rebound
In these niches under a thick layer of blankets
In the cave, we crawl
To wait out the long, long baneful night.

Nostalgia

Greyed shadows of fading gloom gather about,
Rising and spreading
To encompass the universe around
With the reach of the arms to stretch out
and hold, not very far from the bosom.

Glory fading beckons to hew to other times
Written in gold and other precious metals,
To cleave to ancient smiles and pleasant laughter
That echoes through the shadows of time
Clear and unblemished by greasy hands
Of faltering tongues
Of minds crinkly,
And trembling resolve of wilting limbs
Of dissolving spirits,
Who flee the fleeting shadows of night
Pleasant dirge upon rolling vale of despairing souls.

The Unravelling Searing Dream

Dark shadows of searing pain rise,
Incinerated flesh in the dark umbra
Of night smoulders
Puffed, sizzling hot welts of venom pop.

A hot shower to soothe the aching pain
Sweat pouring in droplets,
Of sanctioned bloodletting
Flowing boiling bubbles of water evaporating
To show on the surface as bumps of trapped ooze

Each bump, a face, a familiar face.
Of E. A. Poe. Of Shakespeare and B. Shaw
Drowning in the great inundation of ooze
Melting on the sandy ice of the Kalahari Desert,
A cold, ashy sun hangs in the azure
Impotent on a hot, wintry day!

Time Receding

A bastion of the civilised world
In the desert interred,
Pyramids upon pyramids into the desert sand buried,
Citadel of golden turrets,
And jaunty spires that pierce the sky
Rocky foundations,
And the walls of steel in the mist of time corroded.

Trees, nature's sentries, uprooted
Hurled into the void below.
Planets wheel in silent synchronicity,
A dance across the sky's vast glow.

A rushing sound of sands in the desert,
Whispering to a mirage of men
A tide race whisking a merchant ship
To deeper waters and vast oceans.

Thoughts suspended in a frozen time capsule
Flashing through space,
Shadows gathering beneath
The drooping gaze of a jaundiced moon,
Flickering shadows rushing through,
The fading sieve of light receding!

Befuddled Senses

Oh, vaunted sobriety, my bosom friend
How I have cast away your cloak into the dark
Assumed this apparel of drunkenness wears heavy
To traipse across the floor, wet and
slippery,
In a drunken stupor, I traipse,
A pirouette I make.

Acuity of senses l have not lost, I suppose
Drink does enhance rather than dampen reality
My senses are greater than before, way better
A dust mote I perceive in its full form, swirling
Light in all its spectrum I see beamed across.

But why am I lying on the floor?
And where did my clothes go?
Whose is the river of puke?
Oh, such fetid stench!

Grandeur

I am the hand that guides
The hinges of the universe
Hang upon my command
All planets orbit and revolve at my behest
I move with my consciousness
The entire universe embraces
With love and care, this universe
I have embraced in my bosom
All that dwell in the universe
I have duly accounted for
From infinity to infinity
From the vast to the minutia,
The good and the bad.

I am the hand that guides
The hinges of the universe
Hang upon my command.
All planets orbit and revolve at my behest
I move with my consciousness
The entire universe embraces
With love and care, this universe
I have embraced in my bosom
All that dwells in the universe
I have duly accounted for
From infinity to infinity
From the vast to the minutia,
The good and the bad.

Runesu Chazvemba   Kemet Awakening

I am the ethereal cloud
Vast and all-pervasive,
the building block
Of all with form!

Fading Flame

The light of the intellect burns bright
A bright flare in the dark, it burns,
Lighting the dark night with light bright,
Filling the mind with visions of tomorrow.

Fanning the viscera of the mind bright red,
Igniting an eternal furnace that feeds the soul, churning
out magical designs of various forms,
Painting the world bright with colourful images.

Then amid time speeding forth,
A wind incessant blows, not to fan but to dim,
To snuff the ever-bright glow that lit the dark.
To pull the curtain down and usher,
Where light banished to recede beneath the whorls
Of coiling and rustling, a dark and heavy curtain
That imprisons light in its dark clutches
And whistles an ominous tune of oblivion,
Of a silence so loud that it wrecks the soul
A searing cold wind that burns through the parapet
And the firm wall of Jericho that guards
The mind is rent asunder, and the core is exposed.
Arrows of ignorance vile through the crumbling wall
Come rushing in, each charged with
devastation.
The flame that lit the night long
Recedes and fades into oblivion.

Runesu Chazvemba   Kemet Awakening

The Mind Dancing

Bubbling hot synapses of the mind uncoiling.
A lava, molten hot lava, oozing out of the skull,
Incense pooling in rivulets,
Overflowing the channels of nerves.
Searing thought that cleaves
To a glorious time in eras gone by
The airy-fairy world
Of dreams melting away in a cold storm. The incandescent glow
Of wilting ideals drooping in surrender,
The sinews taut and flexing with a pent-up hope.
Emotions running rampant
Across the emotional terrain. Hairs
sizzling with an unbridled desire,
seeking vent.

Hot, melting and crumbling bones,
Calcifying into powder,
In the glaring stare
Of the bright sun of the mind,
A universe vast, contained within
The cranial cavity, where the mind resides
All the turmoil of being
And all the great deeds unsung.
Receding and coalescing
Into a powerful form, all-encompassing that
melds into one shimmering essence,
The mind uncoiling in dance!

Runesu Chazvemba Kemet Awakening

Raging Emotions

Deep rippling pools of brooding emotions
Dark and alluring energies in the mind riven
Seething heat gathering strength in the bosom
Coiled, it waits ready to uncoil and wreak havoc
Upon the citadels of the uninformed intellect,
That crawls on all fours like a creature of the bush
Waiting precariously to run for dear life, imperilled

Emotions wanton and convoluted, seeking vent
Finding no rampages caroming within the cavities
Stretching the thin walls of the mind taut with angst
The fabric of the soul screeches in futile containment
Of the rampaging beast without form but deadly
An emotional storm gathers strength to lay siege
Upon a tempestuous mind with the fury of a tornado
Whirring and whirling with wanton intent to
ruin

The channels of the mind
And the nerves of the soul flare!

The Mind Awakening

A giant ball of potential
On the small of the back lies coiled A
powerhouse of thinking and emoting.
An infinite horse-powered engine
That revs with power,
Whose vibrations send the universe
Aflutter with excitement?
When it uncoils, it sets in motion,
All the energy orbits of the body vibrate
In sympathy and tandem
With the master gland, the home of awakening.

It pulses with energy and
Life is boundless and all-encompassing.
Filling an existence with purpose
And meaning far-reaching
Infusing the nostrils
With a honeyed, ambrosial scent, heady
The various spheres orbit
In a flash, integrated into one whole.

A golden aura envelops the crown, lighting the world
The mind has awakened
Every particular is within its reach
The universe as a whole
From the minutia to the grand
From the mundane to the spectacular, dust
mote to the swirling mass of stars, huge it
perceives them all in full colour and form.

Runesu Chazvemba   Kemet Awakening

The Man of Ideas

In the age of men and crumbling citadels,
Times of concrete structures
That towered to the heavens
Of gasoline-guzzling vehicles
That profaned the air
Books and parchments
The repository of ideas.

The trains, buses, Lorries, mini-vans and sedans
All these have receded to a fading memory
The world is now in its pristine form of Genesis.
The mind is the driver of all human endeavours.
Men move at the command of their ideas.

The structures now built rest upon ideas
All are predicated upon ideas and nothing
else.

The universe is an idea,
Every perceivable reality is an idea.
All the structures on earth,
A manifestation of ideas
Ideas giving form and the plain established.
The perceivable world in all its glory
testifies,
To the creative force buried within men, to
carve the universe in his image.

Integrated Man

Fractured fragments of ancient times interred
Rippling sands of advancing desolation
Of deserts waxing,
Corroded iron in the rain is flaking,
Detritus for other times,
A malaise of the mind putrefying
under the burden of existence.

In the dawn of a new age, enchanted,
The fragments of being integrated
into one whole, it coalesces
And an integrated being arises.

The right and left hemispheres
Of the brain into one made,
The best of both worlds fully realised
and brought into being.

A new age has begun
Of fully possessed self-beings,
Bristling with a desire to shape the world
In beautiful pictures
Of love, hope and prosperity unencumbered.

Runesu Chazvemba   Kemet Awakening

Within the Cranium

From the cauldron of the mind
Great swords are fashioned.
Flaming hot and glowing from the furnace upon
the anvil of the mind, Excalibur fashioned
This sword is most impressive.

The intellect is the hammer
That shapes and sharpens it.
Great is the hand that wields this
sword,
like a scythe, inexorable it glides.
It cuts a swathe through the dark vale of ignorance
And a highway paved with gold is carved
Leading to Mount Olympus was established
At the peak of this, Mount Olympus
Flattened and levelled is the crest
And a palace of immeasurable beauty therein set.
All this drama within the cranial played.

Wisdom of the Ancients

Oh, the wisdom of the ancients
In all ages stands true
This is true of all beings and saints
Those who rule and those who are kings
In all manners and affairs, exercise patience
No matter the allure
To do otherwise is to be cruel
For anything short of kindness and just
The seeds of discontent in the hearts of men are planted
Further curtailment of liberties
Fertilise the discontent
Tenuous is the grip to power of a Monarchy alloyed
Be courteous in all intercourse with men
Good manners are a credit to one
There is no firmer ground
Than justice and fairness
The foundation of concrete and steel crumbles,
Under the feet of the marauding mobs.
An incensed and bloodthirsty melee.

A Symbol

Tut, tut, my dear child
All is a metaphor, everything is a
Symbol, you are a
symbol, I am a symbol.
We all are!
But there are wont to be footprints in the mud
Tell-tale signs of our fleeting existence
But if you look too closely at the wet mud,

You come face to face with your visage
From whence Adam was spawned, but of course, if
You seek Adam
He lies a few inches beneath your cranial
Subject to an infinity of interpretations.

Runesu Chazvemba   Kemet Awakening

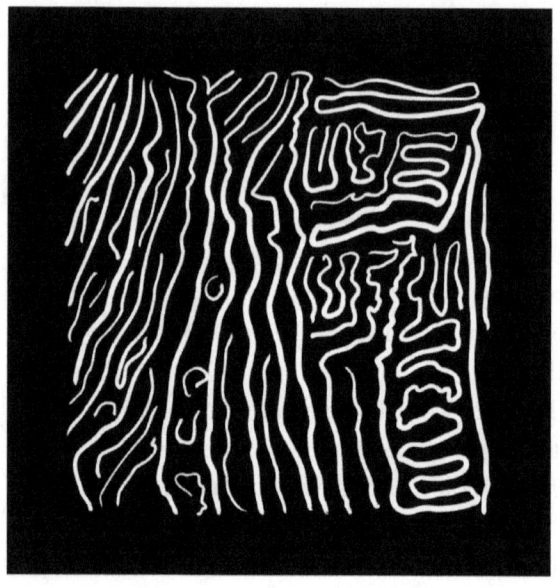

Runesu Chazvemba — Kemet Awakening

The Storming of Heaven

The small things beyond the gaze of man
The substance upon which life is fashioned
In the netherworld, in tandem, fester and grow
Heaven is reticent and in complacency slumbers

Unseen and thus hidden from the gaze of heaven
Growth not curtailed.
Shrouded in the dark netherworld
In tandem, in veiled environments, festers and grows

Once fully grown and bristling
With angst and the force of being
In one rolling ball rises
And heaven in slumber all the while is swamped!

Runesu Chazvemba — Kemet Awakening

The Ascendance

Oh, I have risen
Never to fall in slumber again
Oh, I have risen
From the ashes of the pyre
Never in flames to be consumed again!

Oh, I have risen
From the confinement of the flesh
Never in the carnal enslaved
Oh, I have soared, soared
To the highest firmaments above,
Danced in the starry vastness of space!

No longer a mere candlelight
That flicker and flicker, then it's snuffed
To flicker no more
Oh, I have ascended Mount Olympus
I have become a flame unto
myself, one that burns eternally
and glows without cessation.

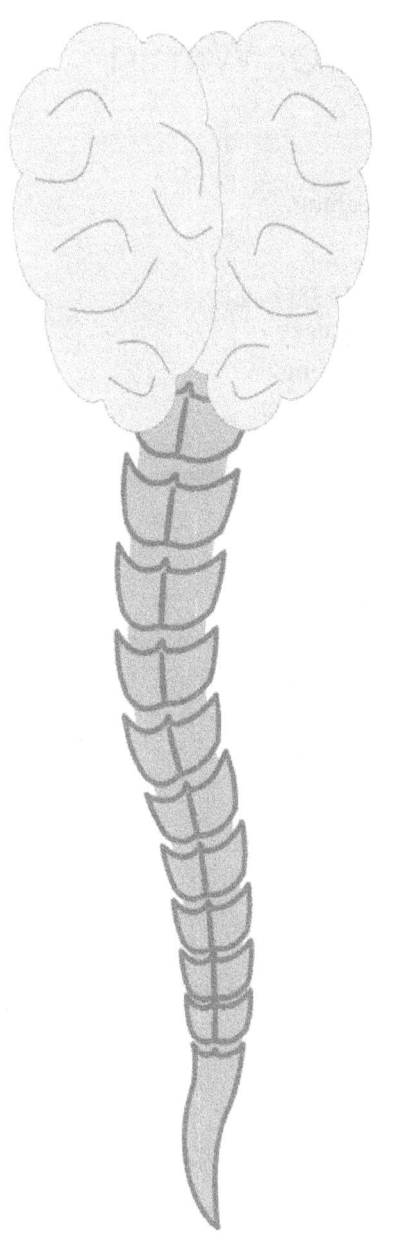

Runesu Chazvemba Kemet Awakening

The Mirror Within

An emptiness with meaning
An all-powerful void
A portal to other universes far
A door to a home in the galaxy
Far removed from the hurtling
Earth, the key to other universes
Resides in all of us.

Hem and haw no longer
Virtue in each set
Jump through a portal set
Partake of the wonders beneath the veil, hidden
All is but a reflection of the force within,
A potent force that moves the universe,
The mirror within the outside world
creates.

Runesu Chazvemba			Kemet Awakening

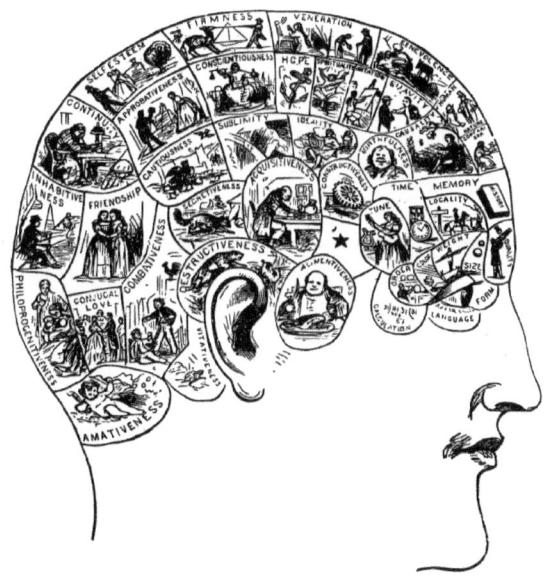

A Hand

A help proffered at the cause
At self-determination to lend a hand
Not out of any compelling plea
Cajoling the able to lend a hand
To the wilting hands and limbs of the indigents,
anything short of full cause a slave fashion
Tolerances of such in the slightest abhor.

It would be better to be slain offal strewn,
Across the vast expanse of space, wider
Than countenance an inclination to pity
A help that enhances the helped
Grows and sharpens the mind of the helper
The hand above and the hand below in tandem rise
Each is a cause in its own right
Complementing each other, and to the skies
rises A Hansel to a heavenly temple
On Earth was established.

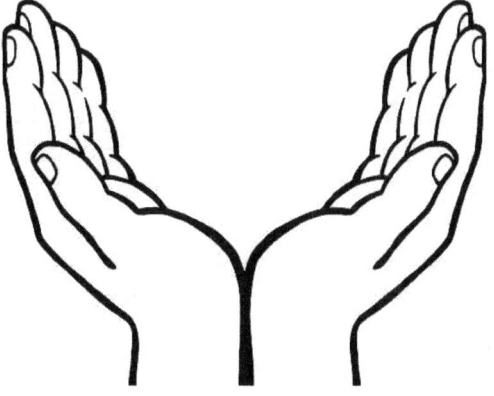

Kemet Awakening

A quintessential symphony pours forth from the heart of Africa, a land where, for eons, the pulse of the world was tuned. Its resonance now fills the world with a melody that sustains life: flora bursting into bloom, fauna surviving in harmony. If there exists a language too ephemeral, the poetry in this work crystallizes it, giving form to the ineffable, unveiling visions of Nirvana, Valhalla, Jannah, and heaven, all erstwhile preserves of the shaman, the Bodhi, the adept, and the spiritually awakened. Here, we plunge into an infinite wellspring of creativity, unfathomable in depth, yet dazzling in its full, radiant splendour.

A scintillating journey!

About the Author

Runesu Chazvemba is a masterful poet, author, educator, and therapist, and is a father of two beautiful daughters, he lives in Durban with his wife Natalie, a writer in her own right. He writes for the sheer thrill of it. He enjoys sharing his poems and stories with others.

Glossary

[1] Orgiastic: of or resembling an orgy.

[2] Maleficent: causing harm or destruction, especially by supernatural means.

[3] Sumptuous: splendid and expensive-looking.

[4] Vignette: a picture that shades off gradually into the surrounding paper.

[5] Amorphous: without clearly defined form or shape.

[6] Attuned: made receptive or aware.

[7] Rapt: completely fascinated or absorbed by what one is seeing or hearing.

[8] Calloused: feeling or showing no sympathy for others.

[9] Besmeared: smear or cover with a greasy or sticky substance.

[10] Supplication: the action of asking or begging for something earnestly or humbly.

[11] Inconspicuous: not clearly visible or attracting attention.

Ignominy: public shame or disgrace.

[12] Subterranean: existing, occurring, or done under the earth's surface.

[13] Kernel: the central or most important part of something.

[14] Bairn: a child.

[15] Depredation: plundering or an act of attacking

Books by This Author

Other Worlds Untold: An Anthology of African Poetry by Runesu Chazvemba

A panoply of poems all in free verse exploring the abstract and enchanting, sublime realm carved in words and drawn with such an abandon and flourish upon the vast canvas of a creative tapestry. The poems beg to be felt, to be perceived through a faculty that cleaves to something ineffable and yet draws upon the effervescent, that deep yearning chasm that only the beauty of sound and word can satiate. It is an invitation to tune into the whispers and resonance of that seat of aesthetics. Having thus been given form with an imagery and form that finds acquaintance with and invites familiarity with a much broader audience, the poems solicit the participation of the reader, where the reader is enticed into and consequently immersed in the sparkling waters of the Pierian Spring and, as one, flow down enchanted brooks and taste the sweetness of inclusivity where all waters meet in the vast ocean of feeling and being.

Kemet Awakening

Whispers of the Dark Race: A Collection of Poetry by Runesu Chazvemba

It is a multi-faceted tale of Africa, unfolding and unfurling its wings, catching the wind as it goes, and soaring to the heavens fully formed and brightly plumed as she rises. The poems are a ricochet through the sacred hall of ancient times, a time when trees whispered sweet tunes and rocks drummed melodious tunes in the night. Man ascending to the highest level attainable. The guitar of the universe, whose multiple strings are strummed by the indefatigable fingers of the mind, the conductor being the soul of man! It takes you through antiquity to the present and soars forth to the future whose plains are nuptial and not profaned by negative experiences of a past singed and a present in

Runesu Chazvemba — Kemet Awakening

flames. On that vast canvas stretching the length and breadth of the globe, a mosaic is dashed out with a flourish and abandon that knows no restraint nor inhibition, but steered by the compass of what is proper. A piece from Europe spun, a flake from Asia, melting on the tongue, hot and spicy. The bright glare of the Americas' smouldering ancient ruins. Africa, that ancient behemoth reposes, the centre piece of it all, the hinge upon which it revolves, spinning a web of poetry and prose.

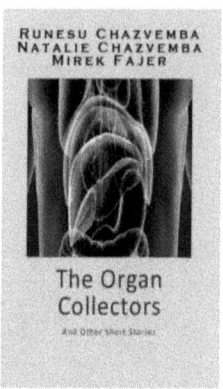

The Organ Collectors: And Other Short Stories by Runesu Chazvemba, Natalie Chazvemba, and Mirek Fajer

The Organ Collectors and Other Short Stories is a collection of fictional stories (and a single nostalgic piece) from a diverse base of authors who came together as a family to express their creativity. Be prepared for a unique experience with every story.

The story, which lends its name to this book's title, is written by Runesu Chazvemba and centres on a man who sought out an eastern religious experience, lured by the promise of enlightenment. When he comes to, he finds that he is missing a kidney. The story takes us on an investigation into the underworld of the organ transplant Black Market, where the most cunning schemes are unravelled.

Be prepared for an emotional response, and your thoughts to be provoked

Excerpts from **The Organ Collectors and Other Short Stories:**

"I was born in the year 800. I was a beautiful child. At least my mother said so. Our home was in the valley of the Perun's mountains, and stormy outbursts of his power left strong impressions upon my young mind. I loved it thoroughly. For all its beauty, the land was rather harsh on our farming family, as mountains usually are. We were a family of five people, which is my father, mother, older brother and sister, and of course, me, Draga." Byzance

"Gracie was six when she was transported back in time. She became used to the conditions in the early 1900s to the extent that her past, the present, and the future were all dream-like. She had once tried to explain that she wanted pizza for lunch. This was met by startled confusion as pizza had not become a common lunch item in Durban at the time." The Vanishing

"The amniotic fluid, like liquid, arrests decay, and the incenses take care of the smell, perfuming the putrefaction out of the corpse. Three weeks in the resurrection tank restores the body to almost its pristine state, without, however, the quality of animation, that one quality which distinguishes between the cadaver and the living." Dr. Melancholia

Index

amorphous, **12, 33**
anchored, **26**
annihilation, **59**
antiquity, **16, 31, 32, 35, 50, 96**
attrition, **57**
Benin, **20**
blossoming, **19**
burnished, **17**
celestial, **68**
Christianity
  religion, **21, 41**
civilizations, **31, 32**
Colonialism
  ideology, **16**
Congo River, **18**
craftsmanship, **18, 20**
cranial, **33, 80, 85, 87**
desert, **15, 17, 31, 44, 76** desolation, **68, 84**
dishabille, **50** Duat, **65**
Egyptian
  African, **18**
Enraptured, **8, 24, 25**
Enslavement, **16**
enthralling, **24**
ethereal, **24, 49, 69, 78**
Ethiopia
  country, **20**
Evanescent, **61**

Excalibur, **85**
firmament, **22, 24, 30, 69**
Genghis Khan's **72**
Giza Necropolis, **31, 50** glory, **7, 12, 16, 17, 19, 22, 26, 31, 32, 33, 44, 45, 50, 52, 61, 83**
Golgotha
  place, **27**
grandeur, **10, 13, 18, 31, 32, 51**
hieroglyphic, **35**
immaculate, **17, 20, 28, 56, 72, 73**
immortal, **19, 23, 29, 49** Impeccable, **8, 27** imperishable, **19, 46**
incandescent, **80**
Incinerated, **75**
indigence, **43**
indomitable, **19, 47**
Inexorably, **31, 32**
Interment, **62**
inundation, **75**
jaundiced, **76**
kaleidoscope, **66**
Karnak, **44, 45**

Kemet
country, **1, 3, 8,
9, 13, 15, 17,
20, 21, 35,
92**
Khufu
Pharaoh, **18**
magnificence, **10, 16,
19, 50, 51, 66**
manifestation, **13, 83**
Mapungubwe
civilisation, **18**
Marionette, **60**
metamorphosis, **48**
ministrations, **29** Mount
Olympus, **85, 89**
mundane, **23, 24, 25,
29, 48, 49, 82** neo-
colonialism ideology,
16
netherworld, **88**
papyrus, **35**
Perceptions, **22**
pervade, **30** pharaoh,
20 possibilities, **13, 17**

profligate, **63**
Prometheus, **8, 49**
Purgatory, **59**
putrefaction, **57, 63, 98**
pyramids, **17, 20, 31,
54,
76** repositories,
17 Resolute, **19, 42**
restoration, **17**
reverberates, **27,
44** sarcophagi, **17**
sepulchre, **25**
Sirius, **20, 44**
soapstone, **21, 50**
sphinx, **44** stele,
35 subterranean,
40 tapestries, **10,
19** tempestuous,
15, 81 totem, **21**
traipse, **77**
tranquil, **24**
treasures, **17, 50**
Undaunted, **20,
22, 38**
unencumbered,

22, 84
Unencumbered,
22, 48,
69 uninhibited, **22**
universes, **10**, **17**, **18**, **43**, **90** unparalleled,
18, **20** Untainted, **24**

unwavering, **5**, **37**, **38**
vestigial, **17** wall of
Jericho, **79** wealth,
26
Zambezi River, **18**

Image Credits

Clipart.org: All the clip art used in this work interior and cover.
dim-gunger-ofgPSZlIaUE-unsplash: cover photo

132

www.ingramcontent.com/pod-product-compliance
Lightning Source LLC
Chambersburg PA
CBHW070452100426
42743CB00010B/1586